CRAFTY KIDS

Fun projects for you and your toddler

Rosie Hankin

First edition for the United States, its territories and possessions, and Canada published in 2006 by Barron's Educational Series, Inc.

All inquiries should be addressed to:
Barron's Educational Series, Inc.
250 Wireless Boulevard
Hauppauge, New York 11788
www.barronseduc.com

ISBN-13: 978-0-7641-3542-2
ISBN-10: 0-7641-3542-2

Library of Congress Control No.: 2006920225

Printed in China

9 8 7 6 5 4 3 2 1

Contents

Introduction 4
Tugboat 8
Space Rocket 10
Airplane 12
Choo-choo Train 14
Monster Truck 16
Hot-air Balloon 18
Big Red Bus 20
Starfish 22
Jellyfish 24
Crab 26
Shark 28
Penguin 30
Seahorse 32
Submarine 34
Whale 36
Octopus 38
Rainbow Fish 40
Hermit Crab 42
Duck Pond 44
Pink Pig 46
Cow Mask 48
Fluffy Rabbit 50
Meadow Flower 52
Woolly Sheep 54
Clucking Hen 56
Apple Tree 58
Windmill 60
Scarecrow 62
Index 64

Introduction

Playing around with paper, oaktag, glue, paints, and other craft materials is a lot of fun. It offers a wonderful opportunity for children and adults to share some really special time together. You will be surprised at how creative you can be.

Getting started

The projects in this book have been devised for you and your child to do together – you do the preparation, read through the instructions, and look at the picture of the finished project with your child, then your toddler can put the pieces together to create his or her own masterpiece.

You don't need to be an artist to create something that is pleasing to look at. All the projects use simple shapes, such as circles, squares, rectangles, and triangles. Animal outlines are kept very simple and should be easy to copy from the pictures in the book. Shapes such as circles are difficult to draw freehand, but you are surrounded by all the circular templates you will need: coins, cups, plates, bowls, and glasses. Look around the house for other templates, such as ovals, that might also be useful.

This book is aimed at two- to five-year-olds, but ability varies greatly within this age group. Although the projects have been devised for the very young, display boxes suggest different ideas for older children to try.

Once you have worked through some of the ideas in this book, your imagination will take flight and you will be able to dream up lots of your own artwork to share with your child.

The projects in this book are all simple enough to be tackled by very young children. Once you have cut out the pieces, your child can stick them in place. It doesn't matter if the finished article doesn't look too much like the picture – your child will have created something to be proud of. There are ideas suggested for older children, too (below) – or your child may like to think up his or her own embellishments.

Using materials

A list of materials needed appears at the start of each project. Pencil, scissors, and glue are used for all the projects, and colored paper or oaktag for most. Other useful materials to keep on hand are white paper plates and bowls, colored crêpe paper, tissue paper, and stickers, adhesive tape, a ruler, and an eraser.

There are lots of exciting arts and crafts materials available, but you don't always need to buy these. Colored paper and

Look through old magazines and cut out pictures of different things (such as the stars around this rocket) to put in your pictures. If you need a picture of a person and have a digital camera, you can print out photos of your child to include in his or her artwork.

oaktag can be found in packaging and in magazines. Scraps of fabric and knitting yarn can be picked up cheaply. With a little imagination, you can give your child the pieces to create a work of art with items that you have around your own home.

Limiting mess

Making things always creates a mess. Cover your work surface with old newspapers or a vinyl tablecloth. Wear aprons or old shirts to protect your clothes, and roll up your sleeves. Use bowls with wide bases so they won't tip over, and containers with lids to reduce spills. Have a bowl of warm soapy water ready for washing sticky hands, paintbrushes, pots, and other tools. Encourage your child to help clean up when you have finished, making it fun, and reminding him or her that everything will be ready for the next time.

Keeping safe

Use your common sense to keep your child safe. Don't leave sharp blades or other tools within reach. If your child can use scissors, make sure you let him or her have only safety scissors with rounded ends. Use only non-toxic paints (ready-mixed paints are best), felt-tip pens, and glues, but be aware that your child might just be tempted to see what glue tastes like . . . after all, it looks a bit like runny icing. If you use glue sticks, make sure the caps stay away from mouths.

Developing skills

Playing with arts and crafts projects will help your child develop, and learn how to follow simple instructions. Gluing and painting help develop hand-eye coordination, and using crayons and pencils gives your child the opportunity to practice holding writing tools correctly.

Projects can also stimulate further investigation and interest. Talk to your child about the things you are making together, look in your library for more books on the subject, and find out if there are any relevant places you could visit near your home.

Staying with it

Very young children have short attention spans and will literally wander off if they are kept doing something for too long. Have everything ready before you start. Some of the projects – where, for example, you have to wait for paint to dry – can be broken up into bite-size pieces so your child enjoys every step of the process. If your child seems to have had enough, stop doing the project, saying you will return to it when he or she wishes, and go off to do something completely different.

And remember, this is fun, so let your child lead the way. The end result does not have to look perfect. Your child will be delighted with whatever he or she creates, and the time spent together is just as important as the art that has been produced.

Tugboat

Tugboats are very strong. They are used to tow bigger boats into harbors, or away from danger.

You will need:

- glue, scissors, pencil, ruler, plus:
- blue oaktag for background
- turquoise paper
- yellow paper
- red paper
- black paper
- 4 large round white stickers

Ask a grown-up to cut out a long strip from the turquoise paper (the same length as the oaktag), a boat base shape from the red paper, a rectangle from the yellow paper, and a square funnel from the black paper. You should end up with the pieces shown here.

Look at the picture of the tugboat and see where to put the pieces. Now you're ready to make your very own tugboat.

Ideas for older children:

- Add red stripes to the funnel and windows to the upper deck of the boat.
- Overlap the shapes a bit and make two mirror-image boats. Use clear tape or glue to stick them on to an empty cardboard box or toilet-paper tube so that the boat stands up. Cut a shape out of blue oaktag for the sea.

1 Glue the long strip of turquoise paper on to the bottom of the oaktag for the sea.

2 Glue the red boat on the sea, with the yellow rectangle on top to make the upper deck. Glue the black funnel on the top of the boat.

3 Use the white stickers to make portholes along the side of your tugboat.

Space Rocket

Rocketships have big engines to help them zoom up into space. Make a rocket with lots of flames coming out of the engines so that you can explore the stars.

You will need:

- *glue, scissors, pencil, ruler, plus:*
- *oaktag for background (any color)*
- *yellow paper*
- *yellow crêpe paper or tissue paper*
- *orange crêpe paper or tissue paper*
- *red crêpe paper or tissue paper*
- *aluminum foil*
- *star-shaped stickers*
- *thick black felt-tip pen or crayon*

Ask a grown-up to draw a simple rocket shape on the oaktag, tear up the foil into pieces about 4 in (10 cm) square, cut a triangle from the yellow paper to fit the top of the rocket, and cut out flame shapes from the yellow, orange, and red crêpe paper or tissue paper. You should have the pieces shown here.

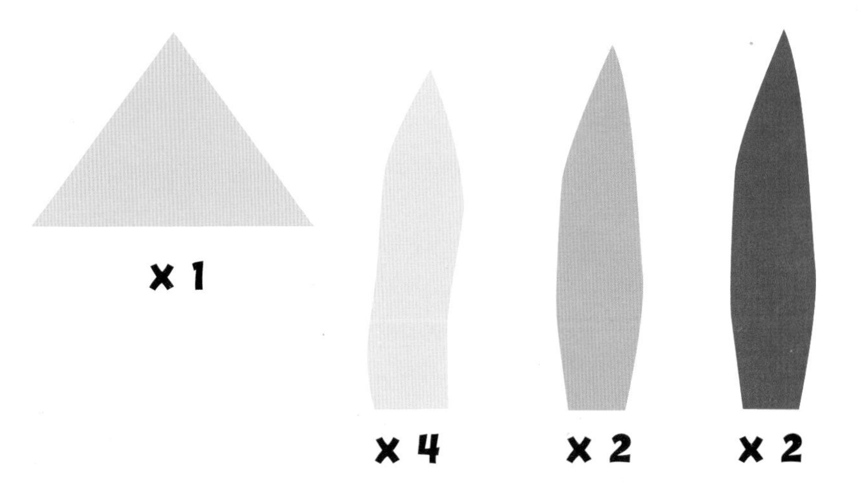

Look at the picture of the rocket and see how all the pieces are put together. Now you're ready to blast off in your own rocket.

Ideas for older children:
- Use black oaktag and cut out the rocket shape in bright-colored paper.
- Cut out three exhaust funnels in different colored paper.
- Draw around the rocket using a silver pen.

1 Glue the cut-out triangle onto the top of the rocket and the flames to the bottom.

2 Loosely scrunch up the pieces of foil into balls and glue them to the rocket.

3 Stick some stars around the rocket.

Airplane

You are going away and now you are at the airport. This plane is taking you to your vacation destination.

You will need:

- glue, scissors, pencil, ruler, plus:
- empty toilet-paper tube
- blue paint
- paintbrush
- blue oaktag
- 4 large round red stickers
- 4 small round black stickers
- 2 foam stickers

x 1

Ask a grown-up to cut out two blue strips about 6 in. (15 cm) and 3 in. (7.5 cm) long from the blue oaktag. You should end up with the pieces shown here.

x 1

Look carefully at the picture of the plane and see how the pieces go together. Now you're ready to make your own plane and go zooming off on your vacation.

1 Paint the toilet-paper tube blue and let it dry.

2 While the paint is drying, make the wings and tail. Stick a red sticker at each end of the long strip of blue oaktag. Stick a black sticker in the center of each red sticker. Do the same with the other strip of blue oaktag.

3 Use the foam stickers to stick the wings and tail on to the top side of the toilet-paper tube.

Ideas for older children:

- Make a larger plane by using the tube from an empty paper-towel roll. Use thicker oaktag for the wings so that they don't bend.
- Add windows of silver paper or aluminum foil.
- Make a tail fin by cutting a long, thin strip of oaktag, folding it in half, and folding back two flaps to attach it to the tail. Glue the two sides of the fin together and glue the flaps to the tail so that the fin sticks up.

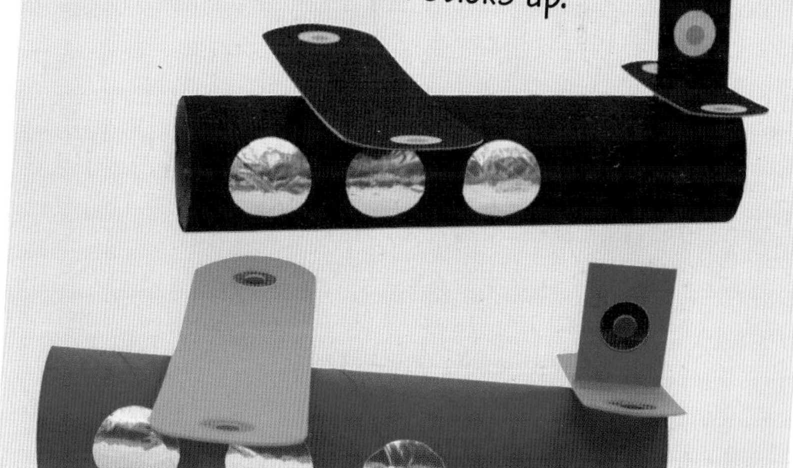

Choo-choo Train

Chug through the countryside in this lovely bright train. Where are you going today?

You will need:

- *glue, scissors, pencil, ruler, plus:*
- *empty paper-towel tube*
- *empty toilet-paper tube*
- *red, yellow, blue, and green paint*
- *paintbrush*
- *red oaktag (to match red paint, if possible)*
- *white paper*
- *round black sticker*
- *black yarn*
- *clear tape*

Ask a grown-up to cut the paper-towel tube into three equal lengths (it's easiest to do this with a bread knife). Cut a strip about 9 in. (23 cm) long and 2 in. (5 cm) wide from the red oaktag for the front of the train. Cut two squares from the white paper. These should be small enough to fit on the red strip. You should end up with these pieces.

x 2

Look at the picture of the train and see how it is joined together. Now you're ready to make your very own colorful train.

1 Paint the toilet-paper tube red. Paint the three lengths of paper-towel tube yellow, blue, and green. Let it dry.

2 Fold the oaktag in two places so that it fits around the toilet-paper tube. Stick one white window to each side of the engineer's cab, near the fold. Glue the cab to one end of the red toilet-paper tube. Add a black sticker to the top of the engine at the front.

3 Thread the black yarn through the insides of the tubes, using clear tape to join the engine and train cars together.

Ideas for older children:

- Make sides for the cars from rectangles of colored oaktag.
- Add black stickers for wheels to the cars and engine.
- Make a front for the engine from a circle of red oaktag. Make bumpers from black stickers.
- Add a plastic bottle cap to the engineer's cab for a funnel.

Monster Truck

Designed to clamber over other vehicles and also used for racing, this monster truck with its giant wheels will make you king of the road.

You will need:

- glue, scissors, pencil, ruler, plus:
- oaktag for background (any color)
- red paper
- black paper
- 2 paper bowls
- gray paint
- paintbrush
- round yellow sticker, cut in half
- star stickers

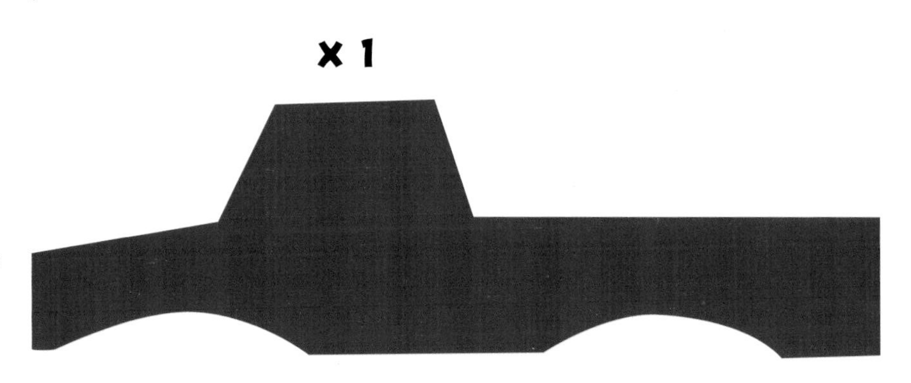

Ask a grown-up to cut out a simple truck body shape from the red paper and a window shape from the black paper. Draw around a circular object that's the same size as the base of the paper bowls on the black paper, and cut out two wheel hubs. You should end up with the pieces shown here.

Before sticking your truck together, paint the undersides of the two paper bowls gray and let dry.

x 1

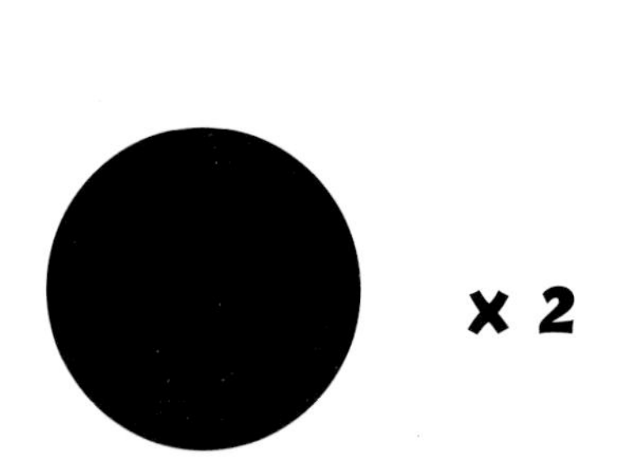

Look at the picture of the monster truck and see where to put the pieces. Now you're ready to make your very own truck with giant wheels.

1 Glue the black wheel hubs to the gray monster wheels. Glue the black window to the truck body.

2 Arrange the wheels and the truck body on the oaktag and glue in position.

3 Stick the half yellow sticker to the front of the truck for the headlight.

4 Decorate your truck with the star stickers.

Ideas for older children:

- Use aluminum foil or silver oaktag for the wheel hubs and window.
- Add two aerials to the front of the truck.
- Decorate your truck by cutting out and gluing on your own designs.

Hot-air Balloon

Up, up, and away! Hot-air ballooning is exciting and fun. Watch the landscape turn into a toy land as you go higher and higher in the sky.

You will need:

- glue, scissors, pencil, ruler, plus:
- blue oaktag for background
- yellow paper
- red paper
- orange paper
- thick felt-tip pen (any color)
- corrugated paper
- paint (any color)
- paintbrush

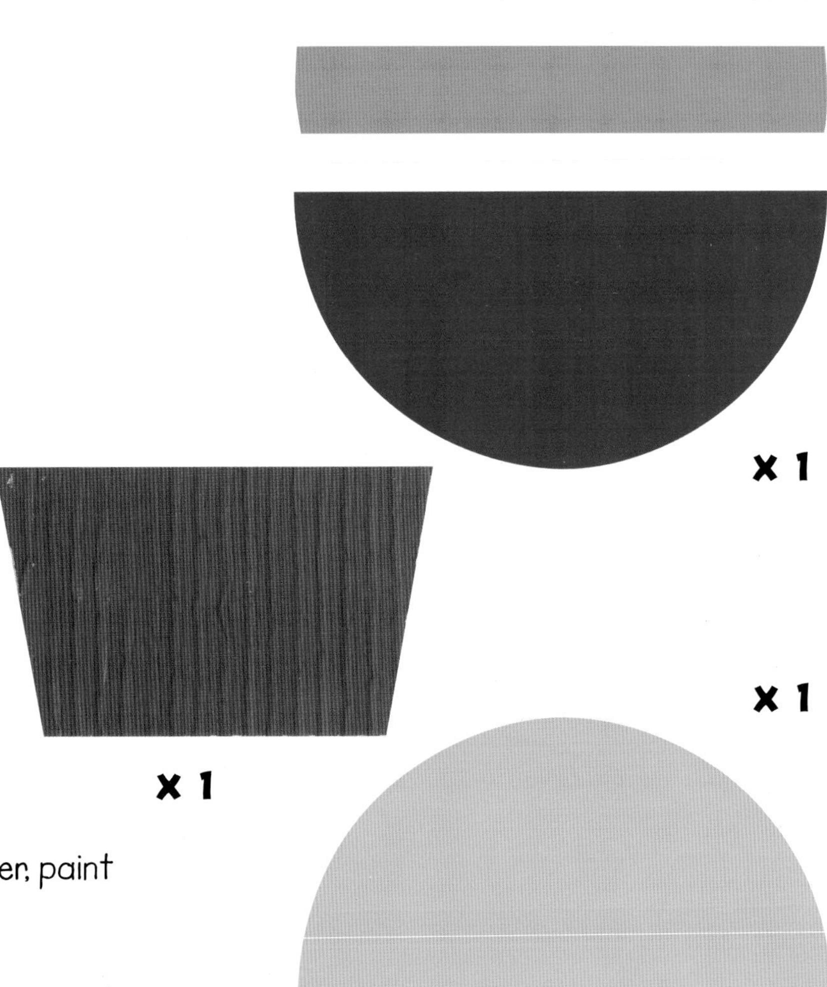

Ask a grown-up to cut out a semicircle from the yellow paper and one from the red paper, and a strip from the orange paper. Cut a simple basket shape from the corrugated paper. You should end up with the pieces shown here.

Before sticking your balloon together, paint the corrugated basket and let it dry.

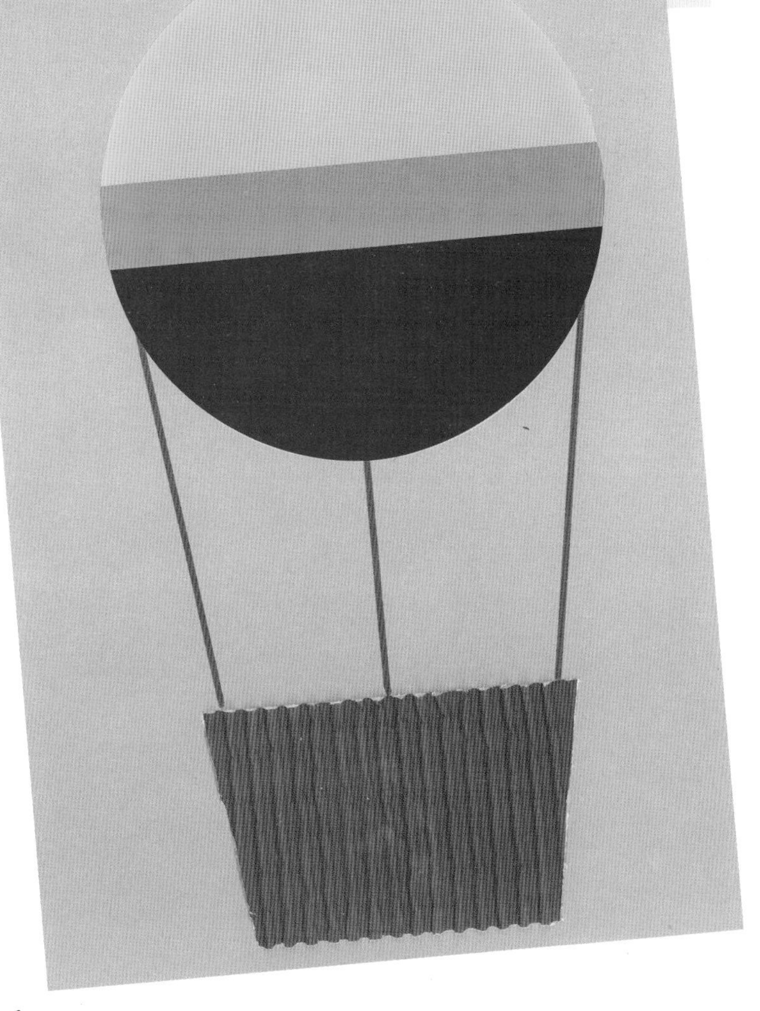

Look at the picture of the balloon and see how the pieces fit together. Now you're ready to make your very own hot-air balloon and float into the sky.

1 Glue the yellow semicircle on at the top of the oaktag. Glue the red one underneath to make your balloon. Glue the orange strip across the middle.

2 Glue the corrugated paper basket to the bottom of the oaktag.

3 Use the felt-tip pen (with a ruler if you wish, or draw freehand) to draw in the ropes.

Ideas for older children:

- Decorate your balloon with stickers or glue on pieces of colored card or tissue paper.
- Use colored yarn for the ropes.

Big Red Bus

Where are you going on your bus ride? Perhaps you are taking a trip with your friends or going to the mall.

You will need:

- glue, scissors, pencil, ruler, plus:
- oaktag for background (any color)
- red paper
- white paper
- black paper
- black felt-tip pen
- 2 large round white stickers

Ask a grown-up to cut out a simple bus shape and a door from the red paper, two wheels and two bumpers from the black paper, and three rectangular windows and one driver's window from the white paper. You should end up with the pieces shown here.

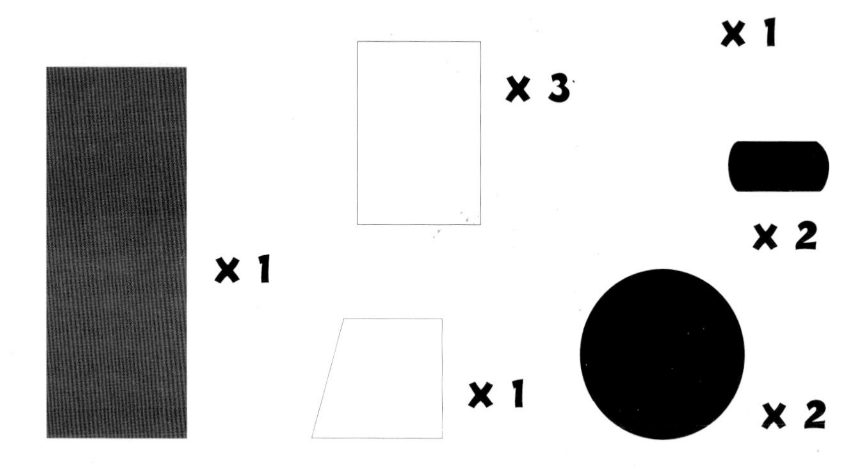

Look at the picture of the bus and see where to glue all the pieces. Now you're ready to make your own bus and go on a trip.

1 Draw a thick black line down the center of the door with the felt-tip pen. You can use a ruler if you like, or draw freehand.

2 Glue the red bus to the oaktag. Glue on the white windows and the red door. Draw a line around the door with the black felt-tip pen.

3 Glue on the black bumpers.

4 Glue on the black wheels. Stick the white stickers to the center of the wheels for the hubcaps.

Ideas for older children:

- Make a traffic light from black paper and colored stickers.
- Use aluminum foil or silver paper for the windows.
- Add a bus number and headlight using colored stickers.

Starfish

Starfish crawl around rocks and coral reefs, looking for food. You can sometimes find them at the seashore. Here's a cheery starfish to brighten your bedroom wall.

You will need:

- glue, scissors, pencil, ruler, plus:
- yellow oaktag for background
- blue paper, the width of your oaktag for background
- red paper
- 1 large orange sticker
- 2 large round white stickers
- 2 small round black stickers

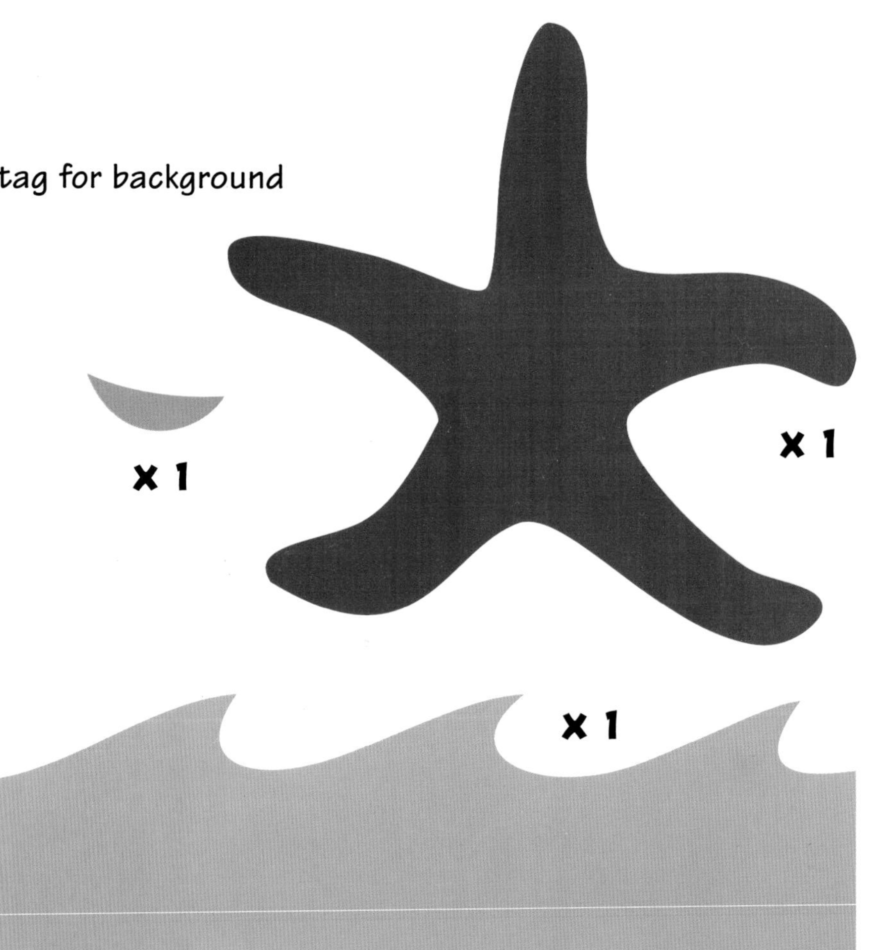

Ask a grown-up to cut out a strip with simple waves along one side from the blue paper, a five-pointed starfish from the red paper, and a mouth from the orange sticker. You should end up with the pieces shown here.

Look at the picture of the starfish and see where to put the pieces. Now you're ready to make your very own starfish in the sea.

1 Glue the sea to the bottom of the oaktag.

2 Glue the starfish shape on the background. Stick on the mouth.

3 Stick on the white and black stickers for the eyes.

Ideas for older children:

- Decorate your starfish with star-shaped stickers or glitter.
- Add some seaweed made from crêpe paper. Glue it on the background before you glue on your starfish.

Jellyfish

Jellyfish look beautiful floating in the waves, but don't touch their tentacles because they will sting! Make your own colorful jellyfish with lots of long tentacles.

You will need:

- glue, clear tape, scissors, pencil, plus:
- blue oaktag for background
- white paper plate, about 7 in. (18 cm) wide
- yellow paint
- paintbrush
- orange crêpe paper
- 1 large black sticker
- 2 large round white stickers
- 2 small round black stickers

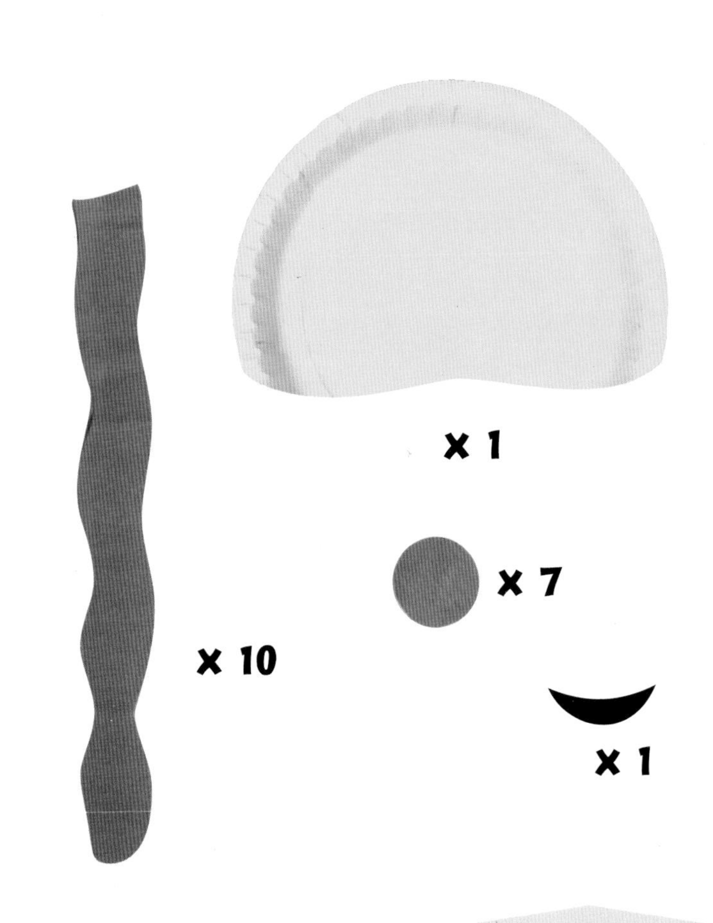

Ask a grown-up to cut off about two-thirds of the paper plate with a wavy edge for the jellyfish body, seven circles, and ten tentacles from the orange crêpe paper, and a mouth shape from the black sticker.

Before you make up your jellyfish, paint the paper plate yellow, and let it dry.

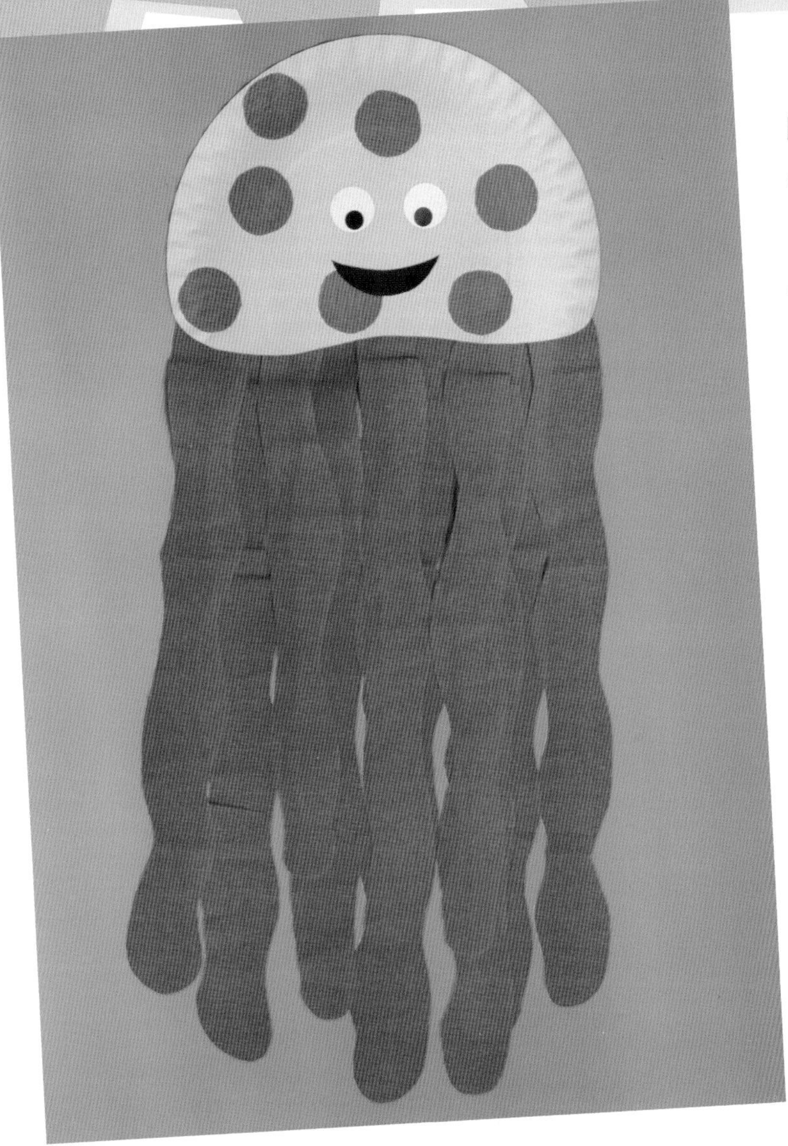

Look at the picture of the jellyfish and see how all the pieces are glued on. Now you are ready to make your own jellyfish. I have used ten tentacles for my jellyfish, but you can have as many as you like. Some jellyfish have lots of tentacles, and others have only a few.

Ideas for older children:

- Use two or more colors of crêpe paper for your tentacles and spots.
- Add strands of colored yarn for the tentacles as well.

1 Stick the crêpe paper tentacles on to the back of the body shape with clear tape.

2 Glue the jellyfish on to the oaktag, with the tentacles trailing down.

3 Glue the crêpe paper spots and the mouth on to the body. Make the eyes with the white and black stickers.

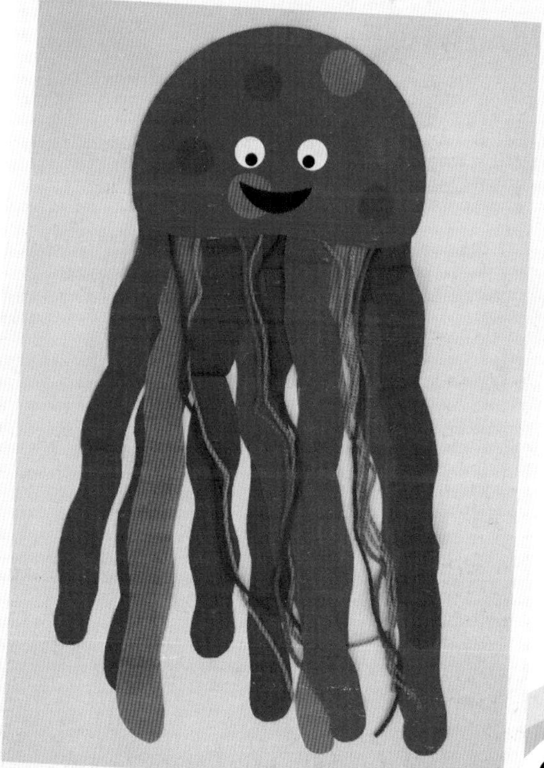

Crab

Crabs scuttle sideways on the sand and through the water. They have powerful pincers to catch their food, and big, strong shells to protect their soft bodies.

You will need:

- glue, scissors, pencil, ruler, plus:
- oaktag for background (any color)
- small paper bowl
- orange paint
- paintbrush
- yellow paper
- 2 large round white stickers
- 2 small round black stickers

Ask a grown-up to cut out eight simple leg shapes and two pincers from the yellow paper. You should have the pieces shown here.

Before making your crab, paint the underside of the bowl orange, and let it dry.

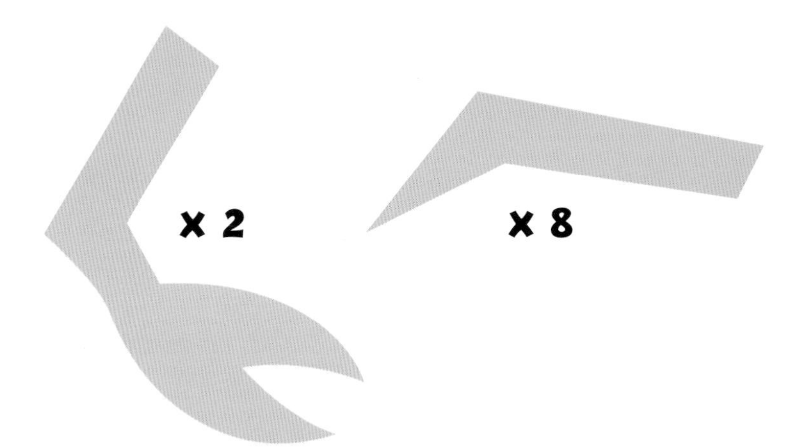

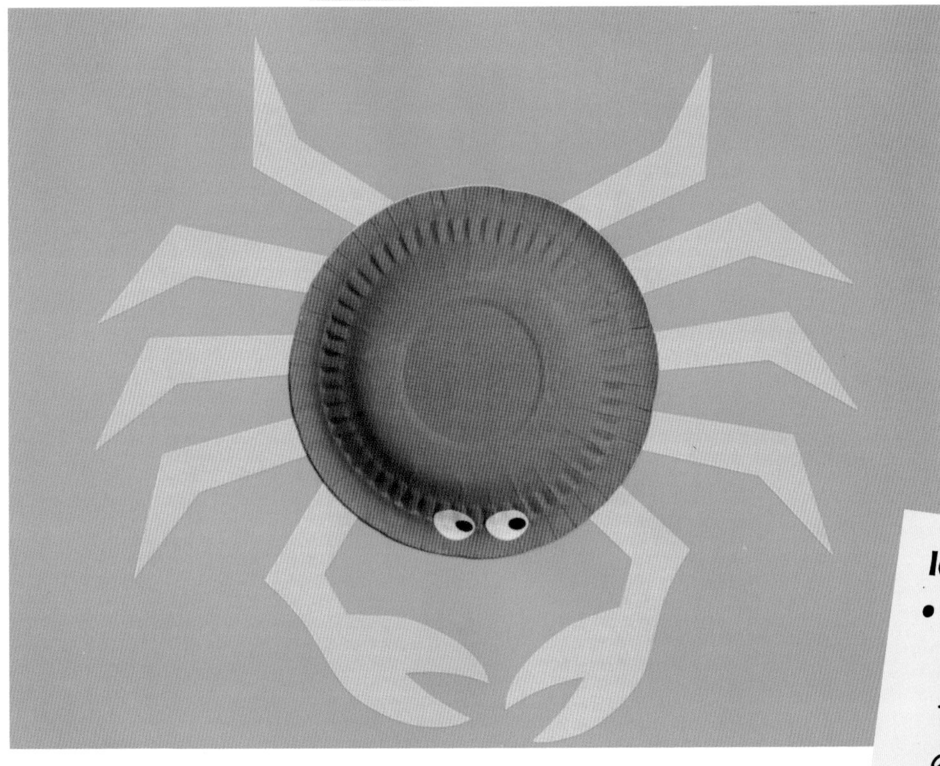

Look at the picture of the crab and see where all the pieces go. Now you're ready to make your own crab with sharp pincers.

Ideas for older children:

- Make some seaweed out of green crêpe paper. Glue it on the background before you glue on your crab.
- Cut out a mouth shape from black paper, and give your crab a happy smile.

1 Put the painted bowl upside-down on the background card, a bit nearer the top than the bottom. Draw lightly around it with a pencil (you may want to ask for help with this), then lift up the bowl.

2 Glue the two pincers and the eight legs around the pencil circle, with the pincers facing toward you. Glue the bowl over the ends of the legs and pincers.

3 Stick on the white and black stickers for the eyes.

Shark

Sharks are the fierce hunters of the sea. They swim silently through the water looking for their prey, then grab it with their sharp teeth.

You will need:

- glue, scissors, pencil, plus:
- blue oaktag for background
- gray paper
- white paper
- 1 round black sticker
- black felt-tip pen

x 1

Ask a grown-up to cut out a simple shark shape from the gray paper, and a shape big enough to cover the shark's mouth from the white paper. You should end up with the pieces shown here.

Look at the picture of the shark and see how the pieces are glued on. Now you're ready to make your very own shark to eat all the fish in the sea.

Ideas for older children:

- Cut out some jagged teeth and glue them into the shark's mouth.
- Find some pictures of small fish and glue them around the shark. Which will it have for breakfast?

1 Glue the piece of white paper over the shark's mouth. Turn the shark over and stick it on to the oaktag.

2 Draw in the shark's nostrils and teeth using the black felt-tip pen.

3 Add the round black sticker for the eye.

Penguin

Penguins live in the cold seas of the Antarctic, diving for fish. They look so funny waddling about on the ice.

You will need:

- glue, scissors, pencil, ruler, plus:
- pale blue oaktag for background
- gray paper
- white paper
- black paper
- orange paper
- 2 round white stickers
- 2 small round black stickers or black felt-tip pen

Ask a grown-up to cut out some ice (the same width as the oaktag) from the gray paper, an oval body from the white paper, two flippers and a round head from the black paper, and a beak and two feet from the orange paper. You should end up with the pieces shown here.

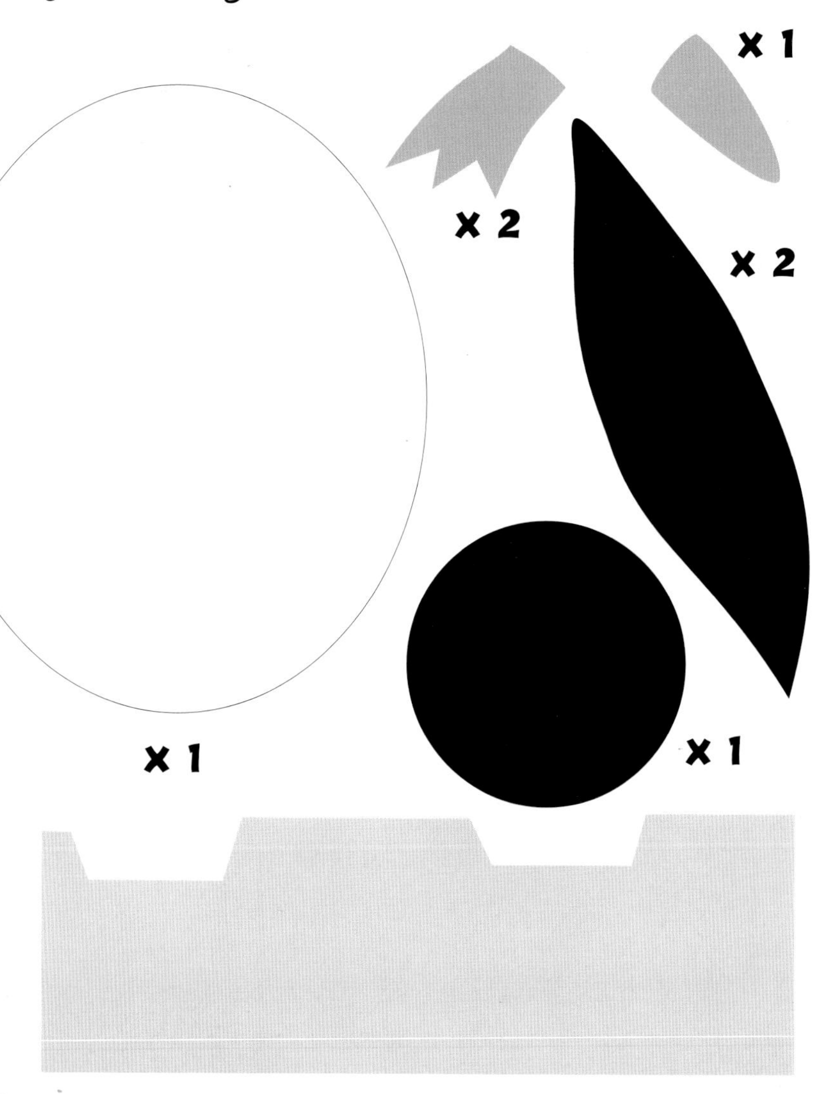

Look carefully at the picture and see where you need to glue the pieces. Now you're ready to make your very own penguin.

Ideas for older children:

- Add some fish for your penguin to eat. Cut out a simple fish shape from different colored paper. Draw in an eye with a black felt-tip pen, or use a round black sticker.

1 Glue the ice on to your oaktag.

2 Glue the feet on the bottom of the penguin's body, then turn the body over and glue it to the background.

3 Glue on the flippers, then the head.

4 Glue on the penguin's beak. Make the eyes with the white and black stickers or black felt-tip pen.

Seahorse

Delicate and pretty, seahorses swim upright through the water. Choose your favorite colors for your own special seahorse.

You will need:

- glue, scissors, pencil, plus:
- blue oaktag for background
- orange paper
- yellow paper
- large round white sticker
- small round black sticker or black felt-tip pen
- silver felt-tip pen

Ask a grown-up to cut out a simple seahorse body shape from the orange paper, and a head fin and back fin from the yellow paper. You should end up with the pieces shown here.

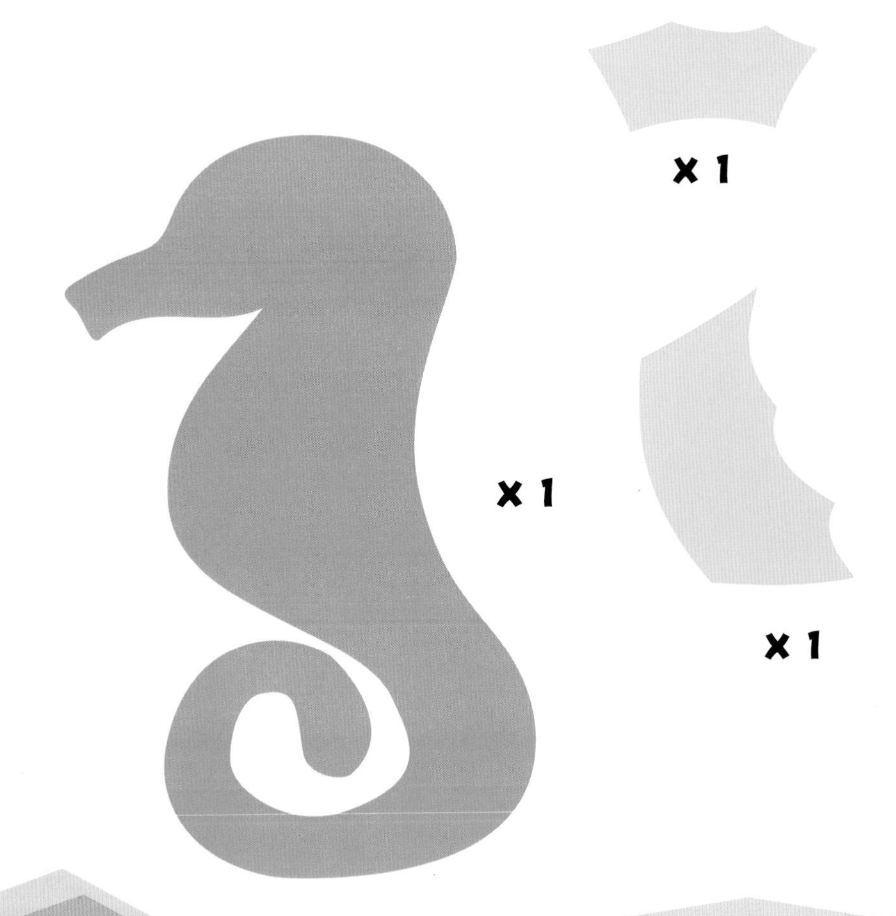

Look at the picture of the seahorse and see where to glue the pieces. Now you're ready to make your very own beautiful seahorse.

Ideas for older children:

- Add some tissue-paper seaweed to your oaktag before gluing the seahorse in place.
- Decorate the seahorse with pieces of scrunched-up tissue paper.

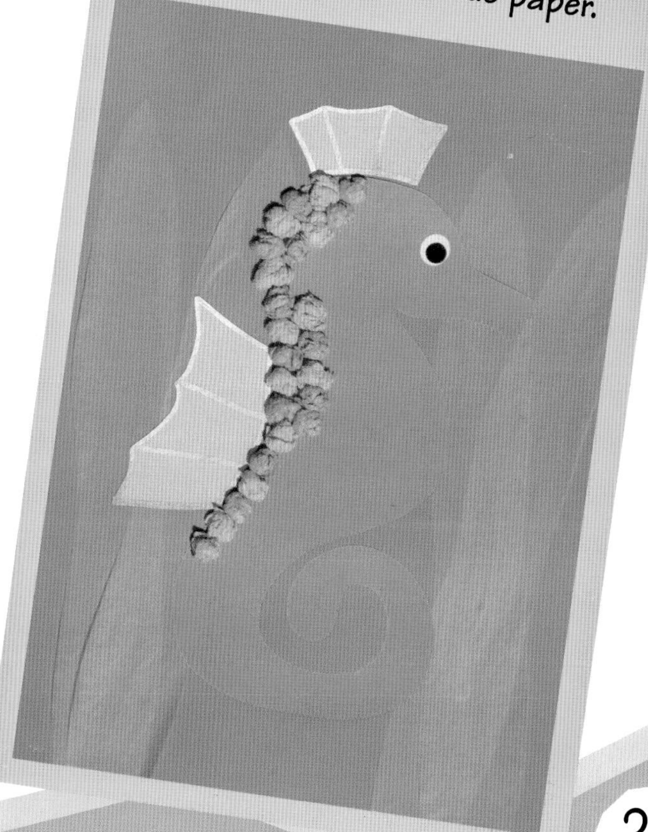

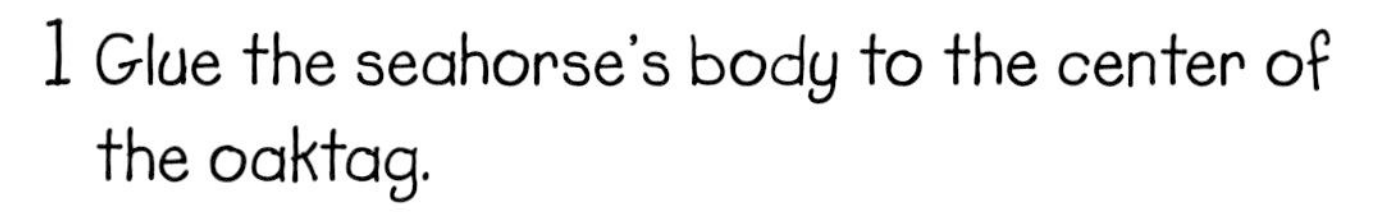

1 Glue the seahorse's body to the center of the oaktag.

2 Draw around the two fins with your silver pen. Draw two lines across each fin from each point. Glue the two fins to your oaktag.

3 Make the eye with the white sticker and the small black sticker or the black felt-tip pen.

Submarine

Exploring the ocean and ocean floor is very exciting in a submarine. What do you think you will see?

You will need:

- glue, scissors, pencil, ruler, plus:
- blue oaktag for background
- yellow paper
- red paper
- silver paper or aluminum foil
- large round orange sticker

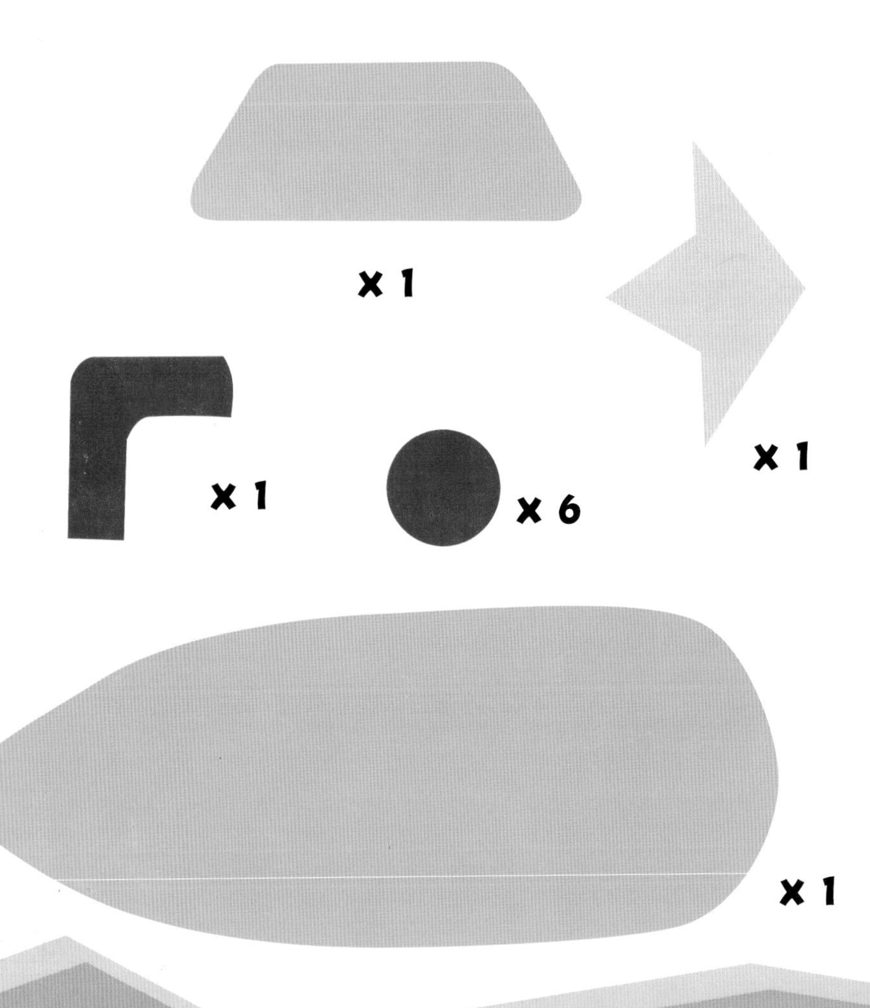

Ask a grown-up to cut out the two parts of the submarine body from the yellow paper, a periscope and six round portholes from the red paper, and a propeller from the silver paper or aluminum foil. You should end up with the pieces shown here.

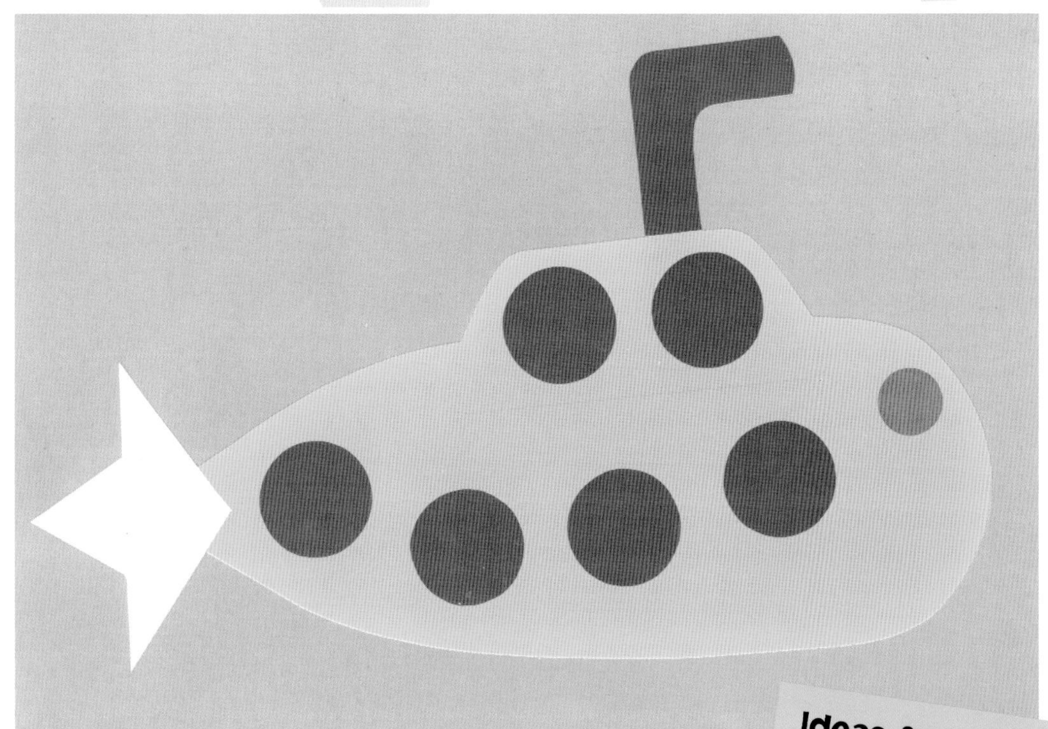

Look at the picture and see where to stick the pieces. Now you're ready to make your very own yellow submarine.

1 Glue the two pieces of your yellow submarine on to the oaktag.

2 Glue on the red periscope and the silver propeller.

3 Glue on the six portholes.

4 Stick the orange sticker at the front for a searchlight.

Ideas for older children:

- Make waves by sticking some strands of blue tissue paper to your oaktag before you glue on your submarine.
- Outline your submarine with a silver pen.

Whale

Some whales are very, very large. When they come to the surface, they send huge spouts of water up into the air.

You will need:

- glue, scissors, pencil, plus:
- pale blue oaktag for background
- purple paper
- blue paper
- white paper
- large round white sticker
- small round black sticker
- black felt-tip pen

Ask a grown-up to cut out a simple whale shape from the purple paper, a wavy shape the same width as the oaktag from the blue paper, and a water spout from the white paper. You should end up with the pieces shown here.

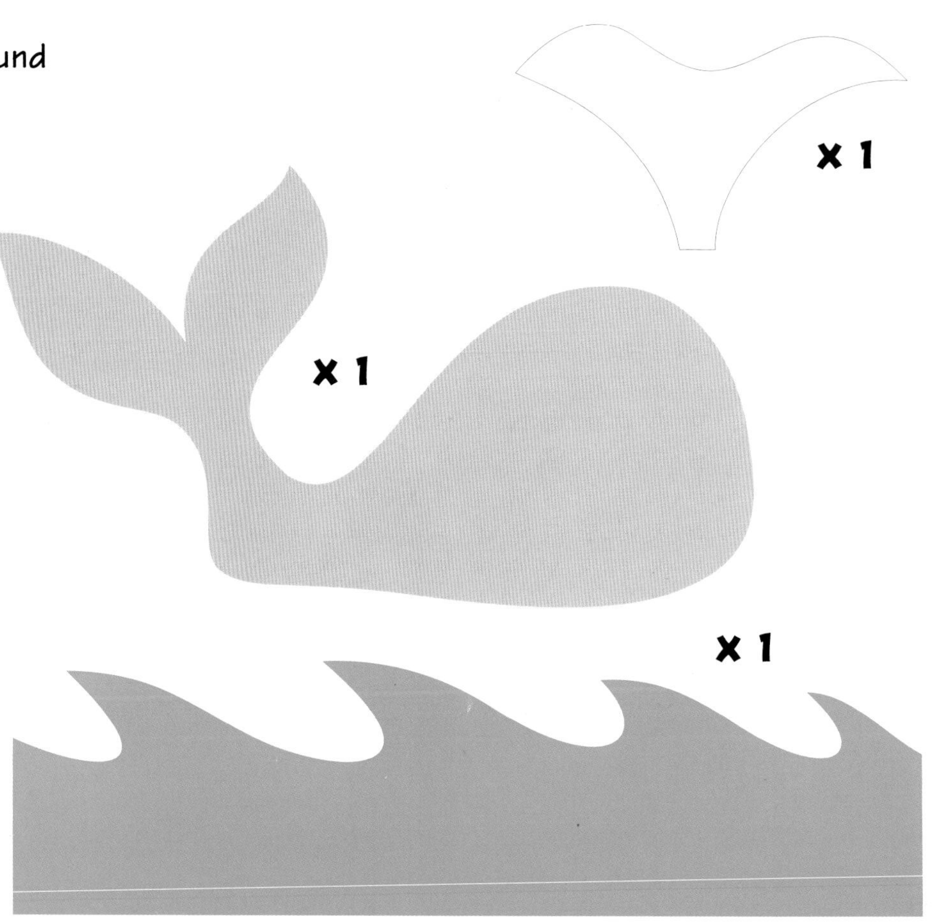

Look at the picture of the whale and see where all the pieces go. Now you're ready to make your own whale with a big water spout.

Ideas for older children:

- Glue the pieces so that the water is in front of the whale.
- Decorate the water spout and waves with glitter.

1 Glue the sea at the bottom of the oaktag.

2 Glue the whale on the sea, and the water spout to the top of the whale's head.

3 Stick the white sticker on the head and then the black sticker on the white sticker to make the eye.

4 Draw in the mouth, or ask a grown-up to help you.

Octopus

An octopus has eight long tentacles which are covered with suckers. Make your own eight-legged octopus with lots of suckers.

You will need:

- glue, clear tape, scissors, pencil, plus:
- large sheet of blue oaktag for background
- small paper plate
- bubble wrap
- orange paint
- paintbrush
- black paper
- 2 large round white stickers
- 2 small round black stickers

Ask a grown-up to cut out an octopus body shape from the paper plate, eight long tentacles from the bubble wrap, and a jagged mouth from the black paper. You should have the pieces shown here.

Paint the plate body and bubble wrap tentacles orange and let them dry.

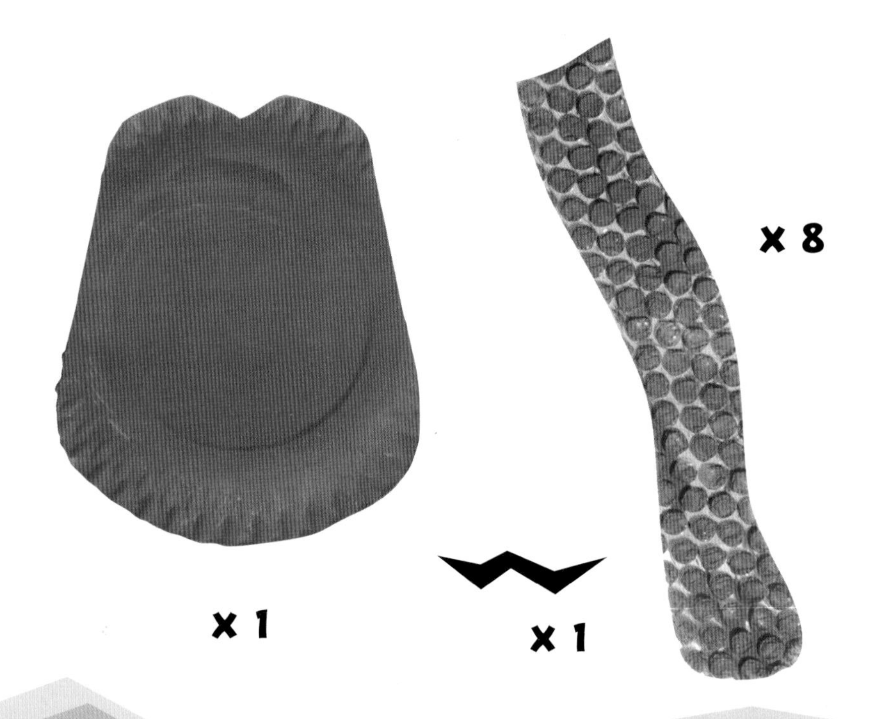

Look at the picture of the octopus and see how the pieces fit together. Now you're ready to make your very own octopus.

1 Glue the eight tentacles to the back of the body, or use clear tape.

2 Glue the tops of the tentacles and the body to the oaktag.

3 Glue the jagged mouth on to the body of the octopus. Make the eyes with the white and black stickers.

Ideas for older children:

- Paint your octopus in two colors.
- Cut a cave out of gray paper and some strands of seaweed from green crêpe paper. Glue the cave and seaweed on to your oaktag before gluing on the octopus. This octopus is slightly worried about what might be hiding in the cave.

Rainbow Fish

Tropical fish can be very colorful. Put this beautiful fish on a window and enjoy its lovely bright colors.

You will need:

- glue, scissors, pencil, plus:
- blue oaktag for background
- red tissue paper
- yellow tissue paper
- blue tissue paper
- green tissue paper
- large round white sticker
- small round black sticker

Ask a grown-up to cut out a fish body shape from the oaktag, with fins and a mouth but no tail, to make the shape shown here. Cut out lots of strips of red, yellow, blue, and green tissue paper.

x 1

Look at the picture of the rainbow fish and see where to put the pieces. Now you're ready to make your very own rainbow fish.

1 Put glue on the oaktag all around the edges of the fish shape.

2 Press the strips of tissue paper on to the glue, so that the strips cover the cut-out fish shape on the oaktag.

3 When the cut-out fish shape is covered with tissue paper, turn the fish over and make the eye with the white and black stickers.

4 Use some strips of tissue paper to make the fish's tail.

Ideas for older children:

- Use more colors to make your fish look really exotic, and use all the colors to make a fabulous tail.
- Add ripples to the water with silver glitter.

Hermit Crab

Hermit crabs don't grow their own shells. Instead, they live in shells that used to belong to other sea creatures. This little crab has found a colorful snail shell for his home.

You will need:
- glue, scissors, pencil, plus:
- blue oaktag for background
- yellow paper
- dark blue paper
- lighter blue paper
- small paper plate
- red and yellow paint
- paintbrush
- 2 large round white stickers
- 2 small round black stickers
- black felt-tip pen

x 1

x 1

x 1

x 2

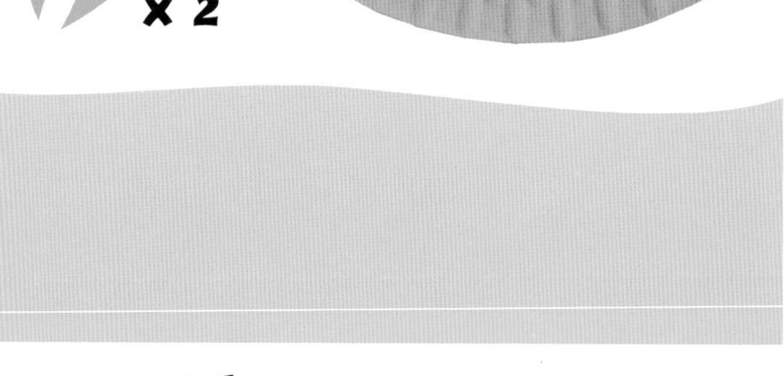

Ask a grown-up to cut out a strip of sand the same width as the oaktag from the yellow paper, a semicircular head from the dark blue paper, two claws from the lighter blue paper, and four shell shapes in different sizes from the paper plate. You should have the pieces shown here.

Before making up your crab, paint the largest and second smallest shell shape yellow and the other two red, and let dry.

Look at the picture of the hermit crab and see how the pieces fit together. Now you're ready to make your own hermit crab with a colorful shell.

Ideas for older children:

- Use sandpaper to make the sand at the bottom of your picture.
- Decorate your hermit crab's shell with blobs of glitter.

1 Glue the sand to the bottom of the oaktag. Glue the two pincers and the head on to the sand.

2 Make the eyes with the white and black stickers, and draw in a mouth (or ask a grown-up to help you with this).

3 Glue on the paper plate pieces to make the shell, starting with the largest yellow piece first to overlap the head.

Duck Pond

Ducks love to play in the duck pond down on the farm. These ducklings are enjoying a lovely swim in the water.

You will need:

- glue, scissors, pencil, ruler, plus:
- oaktag for background (any color)
- blue paper
- yellow paper
- orange paper or an orange felt-tip pen
- small round black stickers or thick black felt-tip pen

Ask a grown-up to cut out a pond shape from the blue paper, a large circle to make two large semicircles and two smaller circles from the yellow paper, and two small triangles from the orange paper. (It's easy to cut circles if you use a glass or cup to draw around.) You should end up with the pieces shown here.

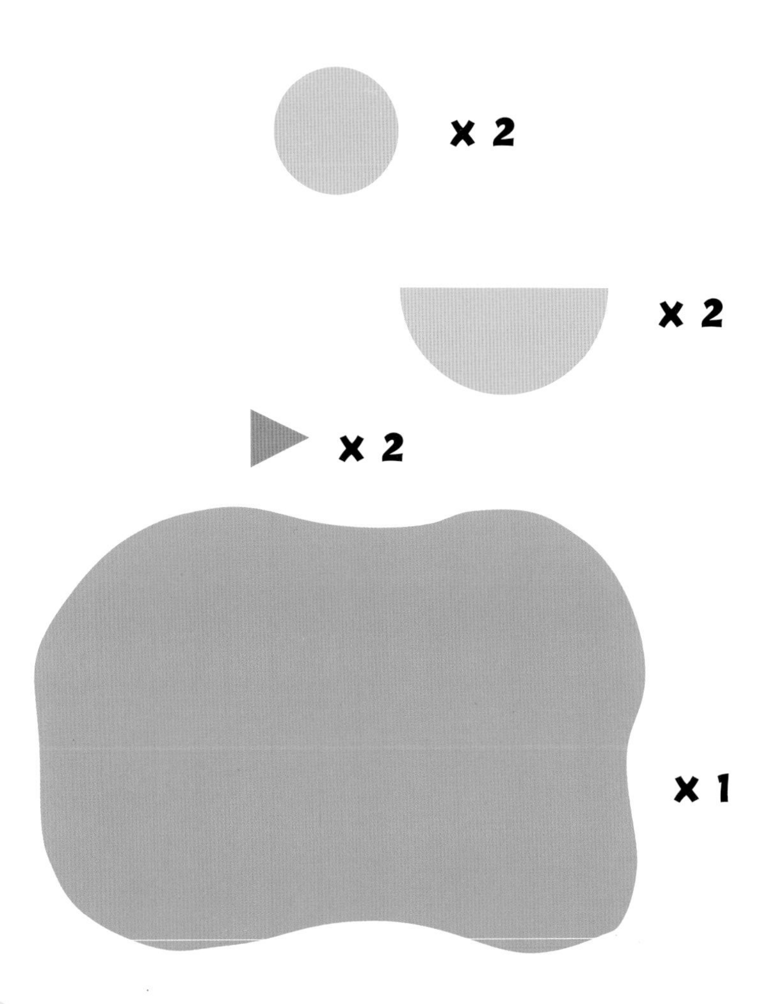

Look at the picture of the duck pond and see where to put the pieces. Now you're ready to make your very own duck pond.

Ideas for older children:

- Make a family of ducks, with the mommy and daddy ducks white and the chicks yellow.
- Add some cut-out paper to make reeds around the edge of the pond.

1 Glue the pond shape on to the background paper.

2 Glue the two semicircles, curved side down, on to the pond to make the ducks' bodies. Glue one circle on one end of each semicircle to make the heads.

3 Glue on the two orange triangles, or draw with the orange pen, to make the beaks.

4 Use the small black stickers for the eyes, or draw them on with the felt-tip pen.

Pink Pig

Pigs are lovely animals, really very clever and not at all smelly! This happy pink pig would look great hanging on your bedroom wall.

You will need:

- glue, scissors, pencil, ruler, plus:
- pink oaktag or white oaktag you can paint pink
- white paper plate, about 9 in. (22 cm) in diameter
- pink paint
- paintbrush
- thick black felt-tip pen
- 2 large round white stickers
- 4 small round black stickers
- pink yarn
- hole punch

Ask a grown-up to cut out an oval snout, two ears, and two legs from the pink oaktag. You should have the pieces shown here.

Before you make up your pig, you will need to paint the underside of the plate pink, and let dry.

(If you use staples for the older children's mobile – see opposite – remember the ends can be sharp so it's a good idea to cover them up; for example, with bits of tape.)

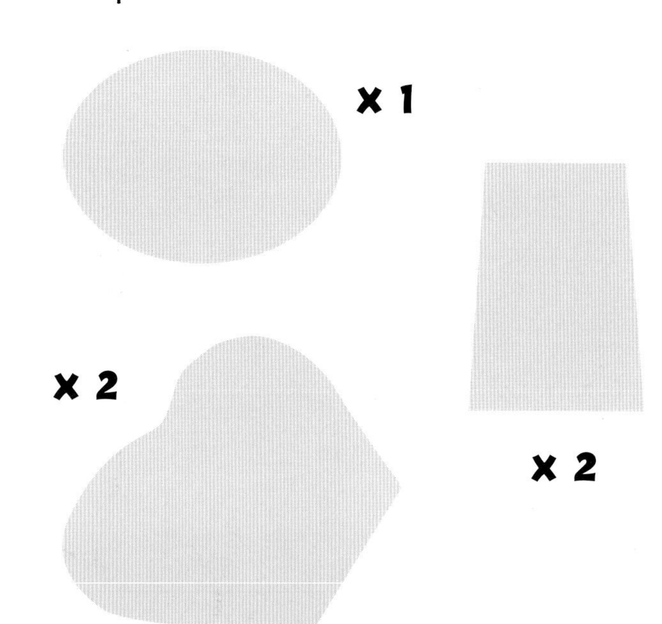

Look at the picture of the pig and see how all the pieces are stuck on. Now you are ready to make your own pig wall hanging.

Ideas for older children:

- Cut a spiral out of pink paper to make a tail.
- Paint the undersides of 2 plates and glue or staple the rims together to give a 3D effect.
- Use foam stickers to attach the snout to the face so the snout sticks out a bit more.

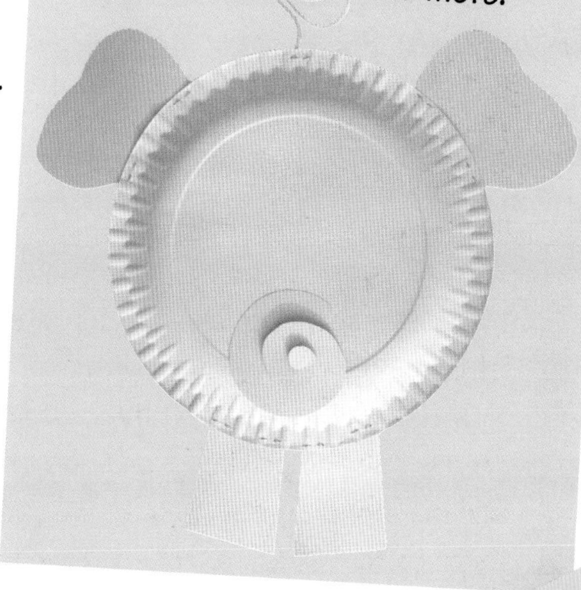

1 Stick two small round black stickers on to the oval snout for nostrils, and glue it to the middle of the plate. Use the black felt-tip pen to draw the mouth underneath.

2 To make the eyes, stick the white stickers to the plate above the snout, and stick the black stickers on top.

3 Glue the ears to the top edge of the plate.

4 Draw a line on each leg for the toes, and glue the legs to the bottom edge of the plate.

5 Use the hole punch to make a hole in the top of the pig, thread the pink yarn through it, and ask a grown-up to tie it for you. Now you can hang up your pig.

Cow Mask

This spotty white cow has a very loud moo. Once you've made it, see if you have any black-and-white clothes. Then you can be a cow from top to toe.

You will need:

- glue, scissors, pencil, plus:
- a white paper plate, about 9 in. (22 cm) in diameter
- pink paint and paintbrush, or pink felt-tip pen or crayon
- black paper
- thick black felt-tip pen
- black tissue paper
- 2 large round black stickers
- hole punch
- thin white elastic

Ask a grown-up to cut out a cow face from the paper plate, and cut two ears from the scraps. Hold the mask up to your face and ask a grown-up to mark the position for the eyes, and carefully cut two eye holes, then use the hole punch to make two holes on either side of the mask, just above your ears. Cut out two or three assorted shapes from the black paper. You should have the pieces shown here.

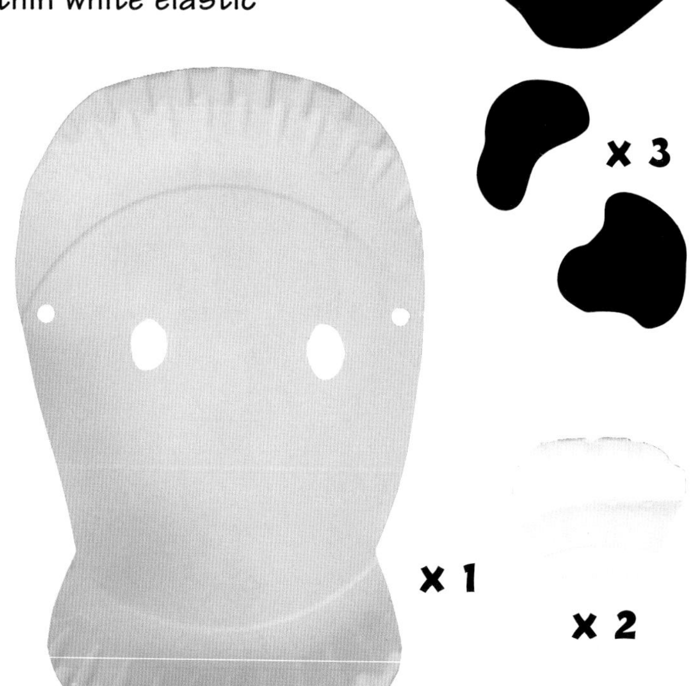

Look at the picture of the cow mask and see how all the pieces fit together. Now you're ready to make your own mask.

Ideas for older children:

- Make more realistic hair by cutting some lengths of black yarn. Tie them in the middle, and glue them to the top of the mask, leaving some strands to flop over the face.

1 Paint the cow's nose pink.

2 Glue the ears to the top of the mask, and the black blobs to the cow's face.

3 Scrunch up black tissue paper and glue to the top of the cow's head for a fringe.

4 Use the black stickers to make the cow's nostrils. Draw on a smile with the felt-tip pen.

5 Ask a grown-up to thread the elastic through the punched holes and tie it so that it fits around your head, going just above your ears.

Fluffy Rabbit

Lots of animals live on a farm apart from the ones the farmer keeps. Rabbits, for example, live in the farmer's fields and hedges. This little rabbit sitting in the grass has a lovely fluffy tail.

You will need:

- glue, scissors, pencil, plus:
- green oaktag for background
- pink paper
- cotton ball
- 1 large round black sticker
- 2 large round white stickers
- 2 small round black stickers

Ask a grown-up to cut out two long ear shapes and two round circles from the pink paper. One of the circles should be larger than the other. The easiest way to do this is to find two round objects (such as different size glasses) and draw around them to give you the shapes. You should end up with the pieces shown here.

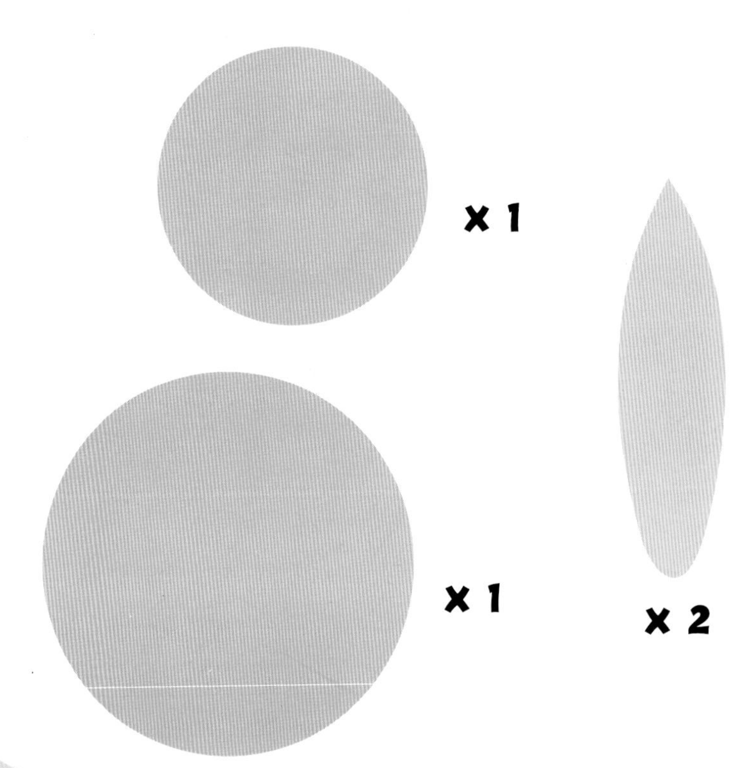

Look at the picture of the rabbit and see how the pieces are stuck on. Now you're ready to make your very own bunny rabbit.

Ideas for older children:

- Bend one of the ears so it flops forward.
- Make whiskers from yarn and draw on a mouth.
- Shred some green tissue paper to make grass at the bottom of your picture.

1 Glue the large circle on to the oaktag, near the bottom, for the body. Glue the smaller circle on to the top of the body for the head. Glue the two long shapes on to the head for the ears (tuck them behind the head if you can).

2 Glue the cotton ball on to the body for the tail.

3 Stick the round white stickers on the head in the middle, with the smaller round black stickers to make the eyes. Stick on the large black sticker for the nose.

Meadow Flower

There are always flowers growing in the fields in the summer. Make your own bright and colorful flower.

You will need:

- glue, scissors, pencil, ruler, plus:
- light green oaktag for background
- orange paper
- green paper (a darker green than the background)
- yellow paper

Ask a grown-up to cut out six simple petal shapes from the orange paper, a long stem and two leaf shapes from the green paper, and a circle from the yellow paper. You should end up with the pieces shown here.

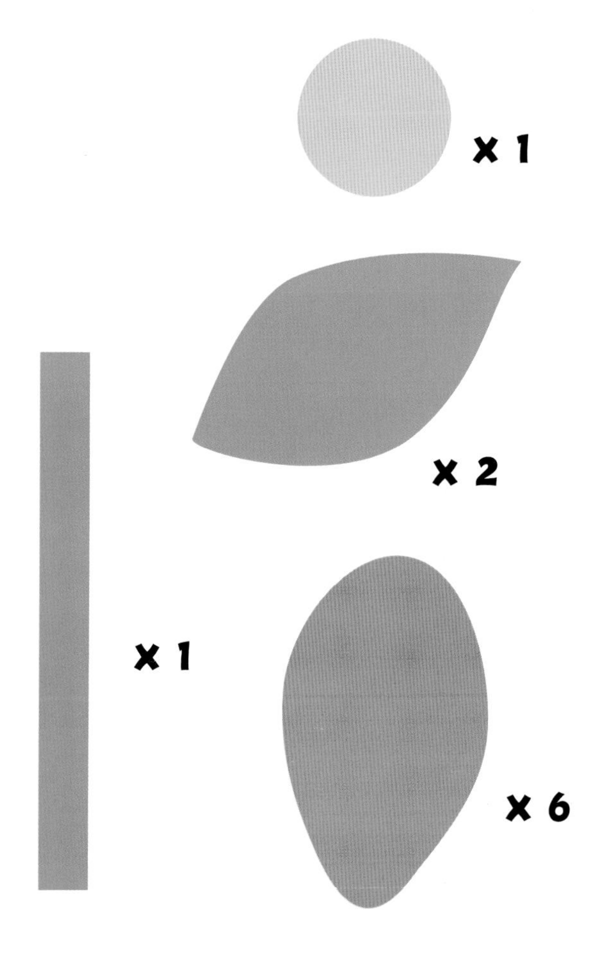

Look carefully at the picture of the flower and see where you need to stick the pieces. Now you're ready to make your own beautiful flower.

1 Glue the stalk on to the paper first.

2 Glue on the petals, then the yellow center of the flower.

3 Glue on the two leaves.

Ideas for older children:

- Make a meadow of flowers by cutting out simple flower shapes from paper of different colors. Glue two leaves on the back of the flower shapes, then glue the flowers on to the oaktag. Use round yellow stickers for the centers of the flowers.

Woolly Sheep

This very woolly sheep loves eating the fresh, juicy grass in her field on the farm.

You will need:

- glue, scissors, pencil, ruler, plus:
- green oaktag for background
- black paper
- pink paper
- cotton balls
- 2 large round white stickers
- 2 small round black stickers or black felt-tip pen

Ask a grown-up to cut out a head, woolly body shape, and four legs from the black paper. Cut out a nose from the pink paper. You should end up with the pieces shown here.

Look at the picture of the sheep and see where to glue the pieces. Now you're ready to make your very own woolly sheep.

1 Glue the sheep's body to the center of the oaktag.

2 Glue the head and legs on to the oaktag.

3 Glue the pink nose on the sheep's head. Make the eyes with the white stickers and the small black stickers or the black felt-tip pen.

4 Pull apart some cotton balls and glue them to the sheep's body.

Ideas for older children:

- Give your sheep a fluffy cotton ball head and tail.
- Add some grass using shredded green tissue paper.

Clucking Hen

A farm wouldn't be the same without hens. It's always fun to watch them scratching in the yard, and to hunt for eggs.

You will need:

- *glue, scissors, pencil, ruler, plus:*
- *oaktag for background (any color)*
- *white paper*
- *yellow paper*
- *red paper*
- *orange paper*
- *small round black sticker*

Ask a grown-up to cut out an egg shape from the white paper, a simple body shape and round head from the yellow paper, a triangle and wing shape from the orange paper, and a simple comb shape from the red paper. (Use the same round object for the base of the comb that you used for the head.) You should end up with the pieces shown here.

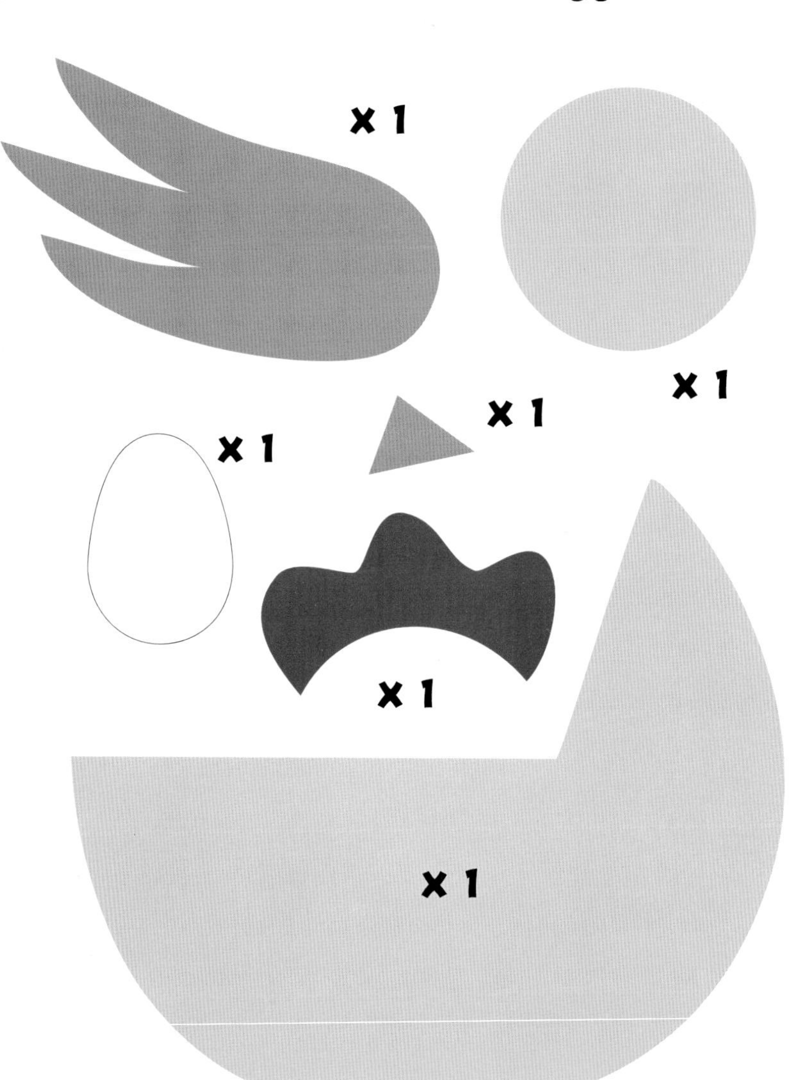

Look at the picture of the hen sitting on her egg and see where to put the pieces. Now you're ready to make your very own hen.

Ideas for older children:

- Glue on some feathers for the wing.
- Glue some shredded tissue paper to the bottom of the picture to make hay.

1 Glue the body shape on to the oaktag. Glue on the head.

2 Glue on the red comb above the head, and the orange beak in front.

3 Glue on the wing shape and the egg.

4 Use the black sticker for the eye.

Apple Tree

Apples are grown for eating and for making apple juice and cider. Make your own apple tree, laden with summer fruit.

You will need:

- glue, scissors, pencil, plus:
- an empty toilet-paper tube
- brown paint
- paintbrush
- green paper
- 16 or more round red stickers
- clear tape

Ask a grown-up to cut out two identical tree shapes from the green paper. You should have the pieces shown here.

x 2

Look at the picture of the apple tree and see how the pieces fit together. Now you're ready to make your very own tree covered in yummy apples.

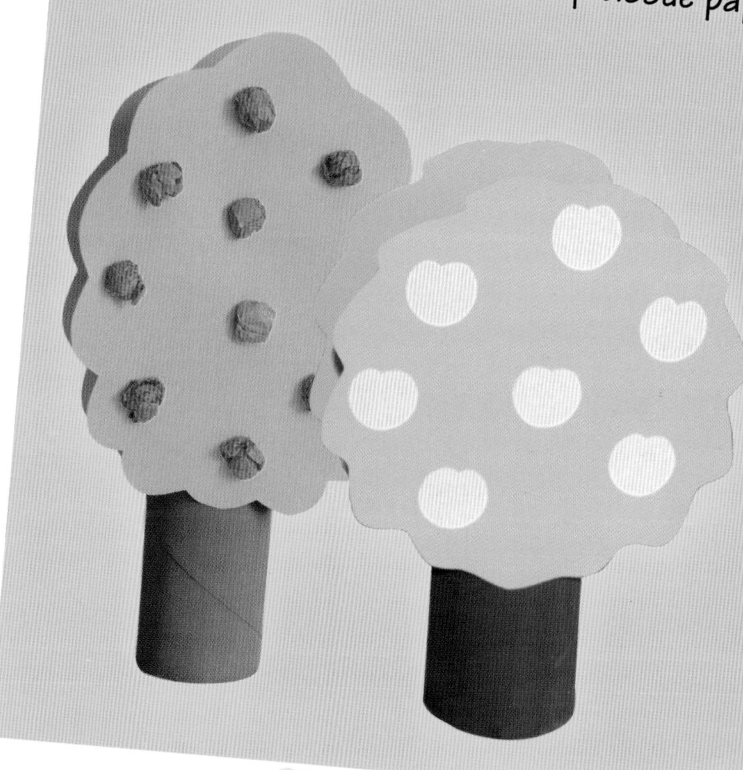

Ideas for older children:

- Make an orchard of fruit trees. Use different colored green paper for the treetops, and make different fruits from cut-out pieces of colored oaktag or scrunched-up tissue paper.

1 Paint the outside of the toilet-paper tube brown for the tree trunk.

2 Use the red stickers for the apples. Stick them all over one side of each green tree shape.

3 Stick one tree shape on to the tree trunk using glue and clear tape. Stick the other tree shape on the opposite side.

Windmill

Farmers used to grind their own corn in windmills. You might still see some windmills in the countryside today.

You will need:

- *glue, scissors, pencil, ruler, plus:*
- *oaktag for background (any color)*
- *pale blue paper*
- *blue paper*
- *yellow paper*
- *red paper*

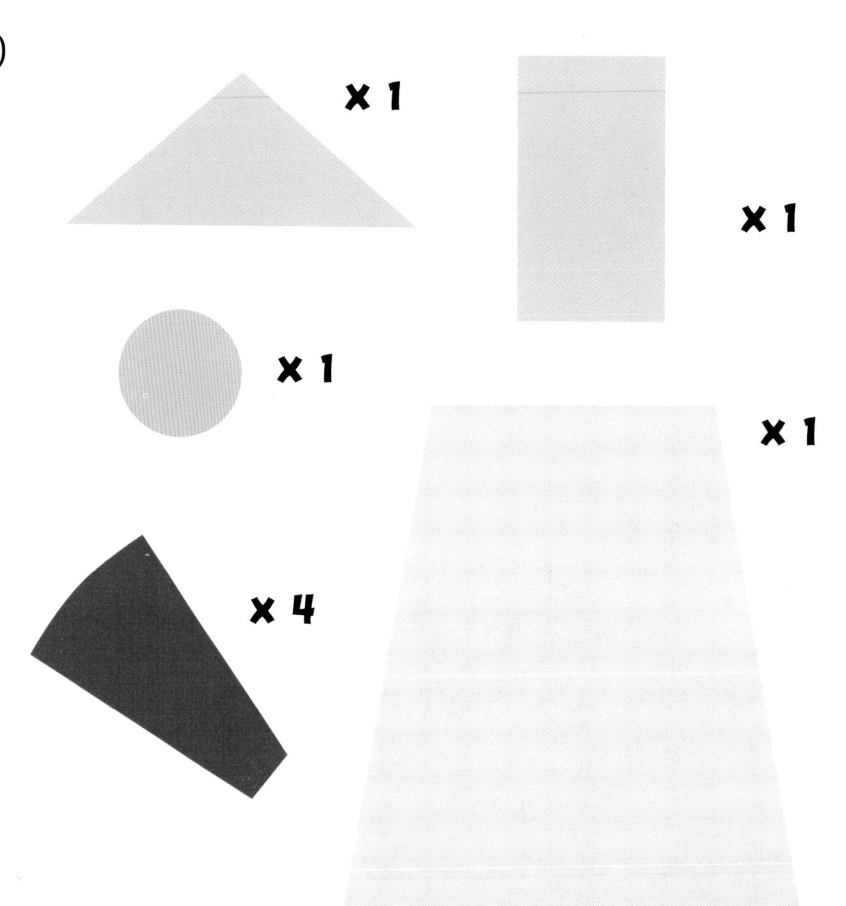

Ask a grown-up to cut out a large four-sided shape with the top narrower than the base from the pale blue paper, a triangular roof and rectangular door from the blue paper, four windmill sails from the red paper, and a circle to go in the center of the sails from the yellow paper. You should end up with the pieces shown here.

Look at the picture of the windmill and see where all the pieces go. Now you're ready to make your own windmill.

1 Glue the windmill on to the oaktag. Glue on the roof and the door.

2 Glue the four red sails to the front of the windmill.

3 Glue the yellow circle to the center of the windmill sails.

Ideas for older children:

- Make your windmill out of oaktag. Instead of putting it flat on a background, glue it together then glue or tape it to an empty toilet-paper tube so that it stands up.
- Make the sails separately, gluing a second circle on the back. Use a brass paper fastener to attach the sails to the windmill, so that the sails can spin.

Scarecrow

When farmers sow seeds in the fields, the birds come to eat them. Help the farmer make a scarecrow to frighten the birds away.

You will need:

- *glue, scissors, pencil, ruler, plus:*
- *oaktag for background (any color)*
- *red paper*
- *yellow paper*
- *orange paper*
- *3 large round purple stickers*
- *brown corrugated paper*
- *black corrugated paper*
- *thick black felt-tip pen*

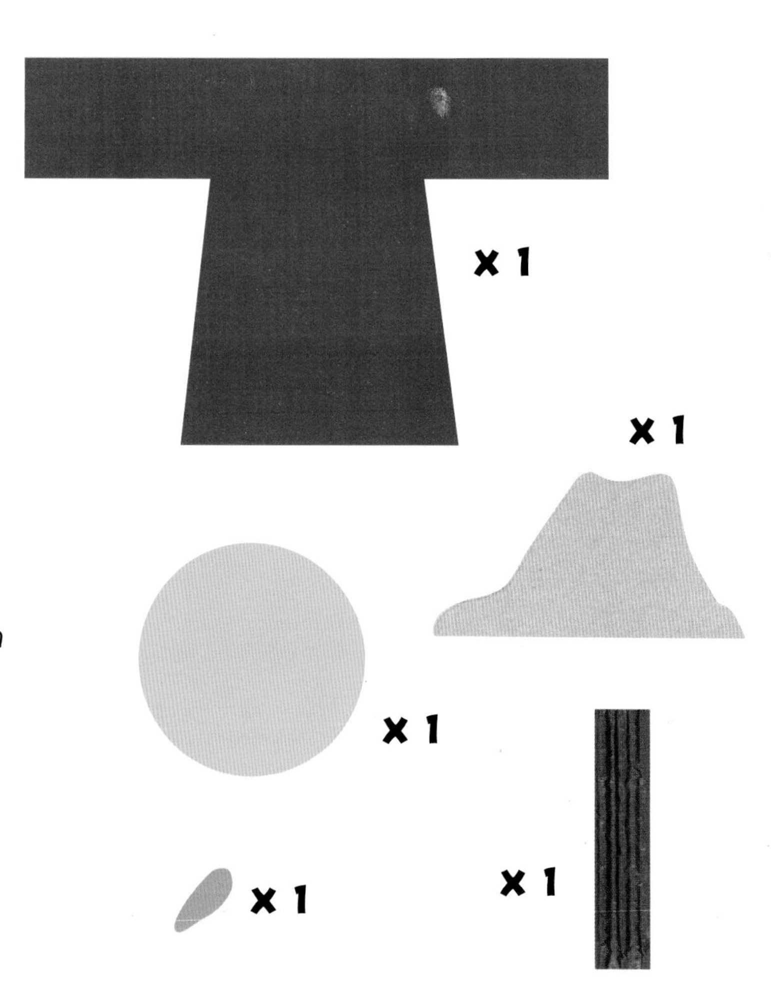

Ask a grown-up to cut out a T-shaped body from the red paper, a round head from the yellow paper, a carrot shape from the orange paper, a floppy hat shape from the brown corrugated paper, and a post from the black corrugated paper. You should end up with the pieces shown here.

Look at the picture of the scarecrow and see how the pieces fit together. Now you're ready to make your own scarecrow to scare away the birds.

Ideas for older children:

- Make your scarecrow's body out of a piece of material.
- Add a feather to the scarecrow's hat.
- Cut out crow shapes using black paper and glue them above the scarecrow.
- Add some shredded green tissue paper at the bottom for the farm crops.

1 Glue the body on to the middle of the oaktag. Glue the head above the body, and glue the post below the body.

2 Draw crosses on the head for the scarecrow's eyes, and glue on the orange carrot nose.

3 Glue on the hat, then add the stickers to the body for buttons.

Index

Airplane, 12
Apple Tree, 58
Big Red Bus, 20
Choo-choo Train, 14
Clucking Hen, 56
Cow Mask, 48
Crab, 26
Duck Pond, 44
Fluffy Rabbit, 50
Hermit Crab, 42
Hot-air Balloon, 18
Jellyfish, 24
Meadow Flower, 52
Monster Truck, 16
Octopus, 38
Penguin, 30
Pink Pig, 46
Rainbow Fish, 40
Scarecrow, 62
Seahorse, 32
Shark, 28
Space Rocket, 10
Starfish, 22
Submarine, 34
Tugboat, 8
Whale, 36
Windmill, 60
Woolly Sheep, 54